Anno Regni

GEORGII II.

REGIS

Magnæ Britanniæ, Franciæ, & Hiberniæ,

DECIMO SEXTO.

At the Parliament begun and holden at *Westminster*, the First Day of *December*, Anno Dom. 1741, in the Fifteenth Year of the Reign of our Sovereign Lord *GEORGE* the Second, by the Grace of God, of *Great Britain, France,* and *Ireland* King, Defender of the Faith, *&c.*

And from thence continued by several Prorogations to the Sixteenth Day of *November*, 1742, being the Second Session of this present Parliament.

LONDON,

Printed by *Thomas Baskett* and *Robert Baskett,* Printers to the King's most Excellent Majesty. 1743.

Anno decimo sexto

Georgii II. Regis.

An Act for continuing an Act made in the Thirteenth Year of the Reign of his late Majesty King *George* the First, intituled, *An Act for amending and repairing the Roads from* Luton *in the County of* Bedford, *to* Westwood-gate *in the said County, and for repairing the Roads from* Luton, *to Saint Alban's in the County of* Hertford.

Whereas by an Act of Parliament passed in the Thirteenth Year of the Reign of his late Majesty King George the First, intituled, An Act for amending and repairing the Roads from *Luton* in the County of *Bedford*, to *Westwood-gate* in the said County, several Tolls and Duties were granted and made payable, and divers Powers and Authorities given, for repairing the said Roads (being Twenty Miles and upwards in Length) and for putting the said Act in Execution; which said Act was to have Continuance only for the Term of One and twenty Years, from and after the First Day of June,

Preamble recites the Act 13 Geo. I.

June, One thousand seven hundred and twenty seven: And whereas the Trustees nominated and appointed in and by virtue of the said Act, have, in pursuance of the Power thereby to them given, borrowed a considerable Sum of Money upon the Credit of the said Act; which Sum, and the Tolls collected and received, have been duly applied, according to the Directions of the said Act, and great Progress hath been made in amending the said Roads; but the same cannot be effectually kept amended and repaired, nor can the Money borrowed by the Trustees for repairing the said Roads, and the Money due and owing on the Credit of the said Act, for Materials and Work done in and about repairing the said Roads, be repaid, unless the Term and Powers by the before mentioned Act granted and given be continued and enlarged, and the said Act made more effectual: And whereas the Road or Highway leading from a Place commonly called Neal's Corner in the Town of Saint Alban in the County of Hertford, to Luton aforesaid, being Eight computed Miles in Length, is by reason of many heavy Carriages frequently passing through the same, become very ruinous, and many Parts thereof are, in the Winter and wet Season, so bad, that the same is dangerous to Passengers, and cannot by the ordinary Course appointed by the Laws in Being (for repairing of Highways) be sufficiently amended and kept in Repair: Now, to the end the several Roads directed to be repaired by the said former Act, and the additional Road herein before mentioned, may, with convenient Speed be effectually amended, and hereafter kept in good Repair, for the Accommodation of all Passengers; and that the Monies advanced or lent, or which shall be advanced or lent on the Credit of the said former or this present Act, together with all Interest due, or to grow due for the same; and also the Money due and owing on the Credit of the said former Act, for Materials and Work done in and about repairing the Roads directed to be amended by the said former Act may be repaid, may it please Your Majesty that it may be enacted, and be it enacted by the King's most Excellent Majesty, by and with the Advice and Consent of the Lords Spiritual and Temporal, and Commons, in this present Parliament assembled, and by the Authority of the same, That the said recited Act, and all and every the Authorities, Powers, Articles, Rules, Penalties, Forfeitures, and Clauses therein contained (except such Clauses, Matters, and Things, as are hereby altered and discontinued) shall be and continue in full Force and Effect, and be executed, as well for the

Trustees empowered to put this and the said former Act in Execution.

Anno Regni decimo sexto Georgii II. Regis. 485

the Purposes in the said recited Act contained, as for the surveying, ordering, repairing, amending, and widening the said additional Road herein before mentioned; and that from and after the Expiration of the Term by the said former Act granted, the said Term shall be and is hereby enlarged and continued for the further Term of One and twenty Years from thence next ensuing, and from thence to the End of the then next Session of Parliament; subject to the Alterations and Amendments only in this present Act contained; which said additional Term shall be, and the same is hereby made subject and liable to the Payment of the Money borrowed or to be borrowed, due or to be due, upon the Credit of the said former or this present Act, for the Intents and Purposes in the said former and this present Act mentioned and contained, as fully and effectually as if the said former Act, and every Clause therein contained, were here again repeated and re-enacted in the Body of this present Act; any thing in the said recited Act contained to the contrary in any wise notwithstanding.

Provided nevertheless, and it is hereby declared, That if at any Time before the Expiration of the said further Term of One and twenty Years hereby granted, the said Roads shall be sufficiently amended and repaired, and so adjudged by the Justices of the Peace for the said Counties of Bedford and Hertford, assembled at any of their General Quarter-sessions to be holden for the said Counties respectively, that then, from and after such Adjudication made, and Repayment of such Monies as shall have been borrowed by virtue of the said former or this present Act, with Interest for the same, and all such other Sum or Sums of Money as shall then be due and owing for or on Account of the repairing the said Roads, the several Tolls, Duties, Powers, and Authorities thereby and hereby granted and continued, shall cease and determine; any thing herein contained to the contrary in any wise notwithstanding. *Tolls to cease, if the Roads are judged to be well repaired sooner.*

And for the more effectual putting the said former and this present Act in Execution, be it further enacted by the Authority aforesaid, That the Right Honourable the Lord Viscount Grimston in the Kingdom of Ireland; the Right Honourable the Lord Gowran in the Kingdom of Ireland; Mark Anthony Esquire, Francis Astrey D.D. Thomas Allen, Thomas Aspinall, Gentlemen; Sir Roger Burgoyne Baronet, George Blundell,   Bullock, Jasper Arris Borradale, Esquires; Thomas Barnard, Philip Birt, George Backhouse, William Bedford, George Barnard, Clerks; Robert Battison, Valentine Beldam, Gentlemen; Sir John Chester, *Trustees Names.*

Sir

Sir Boteler Chernocke, Sir Thomas Clarges, Baronets; Andrew Cross, Thomas Clarges, the Reverend Master John Cole, Archdeacon of Saint Alban's, George Carpenter senior, Richard Clavering, Gentlemen; James Cooke, Villiers Chernocke, Esquires; the Reverend Master Oliver Saint John Cooper, Thomas Crawley of Dunstable, John Crawley, John Coppin, Esquires; George Dixon Esquire, Humphrey Dell M. B. Marsh Dickenson, Thomas Ellingham, ——— Edwards of Carrington, Esquire, Christopher Eaton Clerk, Hunte Everet, John Findlay of Ampthill, Thomas Faldo of Bedford, Gentlemen; Pulter Forester Esquire, Ralph Freeman D. D. the Honourable James Grimston Esquire, ——— Gay of Wilstead, Zachary Grey LL. D. Thomas Groom of Dunstable, Thomas Garrard, Thomas Gape, Joseph Gape, Esquires; Robert Hucks, John Harvey, William Harvey, James Harvey, Esquires; John Hill of Bedford, Giles Thornton Heysham, Joseph Handley, Thomas How, Gentlemen; Francis Jessop Esquire, Matthew Iremonger Gentleman, Thomas Kentish Esquire, Grey Longueville, John Lawson the elder, John Lawson the younger, Esquires; Robert Lamb Clerk, Matthew Lacey Gentleman, William Lamb of Dean, James Lyttleton, Gentlemen; John Robinson Lytton Esquire, Daniel Milward, Samuel Marsom, Thomas Morris, John Miller senior, of Dunstable, Gentlemen; John Miller junior, Esquire, Joseph Newcome Clerk, Sir Danvers Osborne Baronet, Thomas Palmer of Cardington, Thomas Potter, Henry Pye junior, Esquires; Gidney Phillips Gentleman, the Reverend Master ——— Pye, Newdigate Poyntz, George Pembroke Esquire, Robert Richards Clerk, Samuel Richardson, John Russel of Bedford, Robert Romney D. D. Edward Reynolds, Thomas Rudd, Gentlemen; Cuthbert Sheldon Esquire, Hugh Smith, James Smith, Gentlemen; William Smith of Bedford, Pawlet Saint John, Clerks; Thomas James Selby, Hans Stanley, John Strong, Esquires; James Stanbridge Gentleman, Robert Thornton Esquire, Francis Wingate, James West, Esquires; Thomas Walker Clerk, Thomas Walker, Thomas Woodward, Gentlemen; the Reverend Master Wilson Wells, Henry White of Bedford, Gentleman, the Honourable Philip York Esquire, the Mayor and Three senior Aldermen of the Town of Saint Alban for the time being, and the Mayor and Three senior Aldermen of the Town of Bedford for the time being, shall be, and they are hereby, from the time of passing this Act, added to and joined with the Trustees appointed or to be appointed to put the said former Act in Execution, who, and the Survivors of them, are hereby authorized and impowered to put this present Act in Execution; and the said Trustees herein before named shall

and

and hereby have, to all Intents and Purposes, equal Power and Authority to act with the said Trustees to put the said former and this present Act in Execution, as if they had been particularly named in the said former Act.

Provided always, and be it further enacted by the Authority aforesaid, That no Person shall, from and after the Twenty fourth Day of June, One thousand seven hundred and forty three, be capable of acting as a Trustee for executing the Powers contained in the said former and this present Act, unless such Person be of the Age of Twenty one Years, and be possessed of a beneficial Lease or Term originally created for Ninety nine Years, taxed at Fifty Pounds per Annum, or more, above the reserved Rent upon such Lease, or is seized or possessed for his Life or some greater Estate, to his own Use, of Lands, Tenements, or Hereditaments, which were taxed for Fifty Pounds per Annum, or more, in the Counties of Bedford and Hertford, towards raising the Land-tax for the Year One thousand seven hundred and forty two, or which shall be so taxed as aforesaid for any Year or Years, in which such Person shall as aforesaid act as a Trustee for putting the said former and this present Act in Execution; or that such Person is or shall be Heir Apparent to some Person, who shall be seized of Lands, Tenements, or Hereditaments in the said Counties of Bedford or Hertford, taxed at One hundred Pounds per Annum (except the Mayor and Three senior Aldermen of the Town of Bedford for the time being, and the Mayor and Three senior Aldermen of the Town of Saint Alban, in the said County of Hertford, for the time being) and the respective Qualifications before mentioned shall be proved upon the Oath of the Party, if thereunto required by the said Trustees for putting the said former and this present Act in Execution, or any Five or more of them (which Oath One or more of the said Trustees is and are hereby impowered to administer) And if any Person, not being so qualified as aforesaid, shall, after the said Twenty fourth Day of June, One thousand seven hundred and forty three, act as a Trustee for the Purposes in the said former and this present Act mentioned, or shall do any Act as such Trustee, contrary to the Intent and true Meaning hereof, the Person so offending shall, for every such Act or Offence, forfeit and pay the Sum of Twenty Shillings to such Person or Persons as shall sue for the same; to be recovered by Action of Debt, Bill, Plaint, or Information, in any of His Majesty's Courts of Record at Westminster, wherein no Essoin, Protection, Privilege,

Qualification of Trustees.

lege, or Wager of Law, or more than one Imparlance shall be allowed; One Moiety of the said last mentioned Penalty shall go to such Person or Persons who shall sue for the same, and the other Moiety thereof shall be laid out and applied for and towards amending the Roads directed to be repaired by the said former and this present Act, and for no other Use or Purpose whatsoever.

Trustees to have two fixed Meetings yearly.

And it is hereby further enacted by the Authority aforesaid, That from and after the passing of this Act, the said Trustees appointed or to be appointed to put the said former and this present Act in Execution, shall have Two fixed General Meetings yearly; that is to say, One whereof shall be held at the Town of Bedford, and the other at Luton in the said County of Bedford; and that the First General Meeting of the said Trustees shall be on the First Tuesday after the First Day of May, One thousand seven hundred and forty three, at the Bell Inn in the Town of Bedford; and the Second Meeting of the said Trustees shall be at the George Inn in Luton aforesaid, on the Tuesday next before Michaelmas-day next coming; and so alternately, one Meeting shall be at some convenient House in the said Town of Bedford on Tuesday in Easter Week yearly, and one Meeting at some convenient House in Luton aforesaid, on the Tuesday next before Michaelmas-day yearly, during the Continuance of the said former and this present Act, as the said Trustees at such General Meetings, or the major Part of them then present, shall order and appoint.

Clause for reducing the Number of Trustees to act.

And whereas the Trustees appointed to put the said former Act in Execution are, in several Cases, restrained from acting, unless Nine or more of them are present at their Meetings, which has by Experience been found very inconvenient: Be it therefore enacted by the Authority aforesaid, That from and after the passing of this Act, any Five or more of the Trustees appointed or to be appointed to put the said former and this present Act in Execution, shall, and they are hereby impowered to act, where Nine or more of the said Trustees are by the said former Act required to act; except in such Cases when any Money is to be borrowed on the Credit of the said former and this present Act, or at the Election of any new Trustee or Trustees for putting the said Acts in Execution, in the Room of such Trustee or Trustees as shall hereafter die, remove, or refuse to act; any thing in the said former Act contained to the contrary notwithstanding.

Anno Regni decimo sexto Georgii II. Regis.

And be it further enacted and declared by the Authority aforesaid, That if it shall happen at any time after the passing of this Act, and during the Continuance of the said former and this present Act, there shall not appear at any Meeting, which shall be appointed to be held by the said Trustees, a sufficient Number of them to act at such Meeting, and to adjourn to another time; or in case the said Trustees shall neglect to make a proper Adjournment; in such Case or Cases respectively, the Clerk to the said Trustees, (which Clerk the said Trustees, or any Five or more of them, are hereby impowered to nominate and appoint) shall, and he is hereby required to appoint another Meeting of the said Trustees, by affixing publick Notice under his Hand, at or upon all the Turnpike-gates erected, or to be erected, by virtue of the said former and this present Act, at least Ten Days before such next Meeting; which Meeting shall be held at some convenient House near the said Roads on that Day Month after such Neglect of the Meeting or Adjournment of the said Trustees.

The Clerk to appoint another Meeting of the Trustees, if a sufficient Number do not appear.

Provided also, and be it further enacted by the Authority aforesaid, That all the Turnpikes and Toll-houses erected in pursuance of the said former Act, cross or in the said Roads directed to be repaired by the said former Act, at the Places called Saint Mary's in the Town of Bedford aforesaid, and at Luton Town's End, shall, within One Month after the First Meeting of the Trustees, to be held after the passing of this Act, be pulled down and taken away; and that no Turnpike or Toll-house shall, during the Continuance of the said former and this present Act, be erected or set up between a Place called Elvestow alias Elstow, in the said County of Bedford, and a Mile North of the said Town of Bedford, nor within One Mile of the Town of Luton aforesaid.

Clauses to pull down Turnpikes, and erect new ones.

Provided also, and be it further enacted by the Authority aforesaid, That it shall and may be lawful to and for the said Trustees, or any Five or more of them, as soon as may be, after the First Meeting of the said Trustees to be held after the passing of this Act, to erect, or cause to be erected or set up, the said Turnpikes and Tollhouses herein before directed to be pulled down and taken away, or any new Turnpike and Tollhouse in, cross, or on the Sides of the Road between Saint Alban's and one Mile of the Town of Luton aforesaid, at such Places as the said Trustees, or the major Part of them, at their First publick Meeting, to be held after the passing of this Act, shall order and direct, so as the same be not set up within Four Miles of the Town of Saint Alban aforesaid;

and all and every Person and Persons travelling or passing through the said last mentioned Turnpike, shall pay the several Tolls granted and made payable by the said former, and continued by this present Act, in such Manner and Form as the said former Act directs, unless such Person or Persons shall have paid the said Tolls before at any other Turnpike erected or to be erected between Elstow and One Mile of the Town of Luton aforesaid.

And be it further enacted by the Authority aforesaid, That the Turnpike-gate now standing in the Parish of Hawnes in the said County of Bedford, shall remain where the same is now erected, or shall be removed to such other Place between Elvestow otherwise Elstow aforesaid, and One Mile North of Luton aforesaid, as the said Trustees, or the major Part of them, shall, at any General Meeting order and direct; but no Toll shall be paid by any Person or Persons passing through the said Turnpike, in the Parish of Hawnes aforesaid, in case such Person or Persons shall have paid the Toll before, and producing a Ticket or Tickets signifying the Payment of the said Toll at any Turnpike erected or to be erected, between Luton and Saint Alban's aforesaid; nor shall any Toll be paid by any Person or Persons passing through any Turnpike, which shall be erected or set up between Saint Alban's and Luton aforesaid, in case such Person or Persons shall have paid the Toll before, and producing a Ticket or Tickets, signifying the Payment of the said Toll at any Turnpike erected or to be erected between Elstow and Luton aforesaid; but no such Payment shall exempt any such Person or Persons from paying the Toll by the said former Act granted, and hereby continued, at any Gate or Turnpike erected or to be erected on the North Side of the River Ouze; but the Gates or Turnpikes erected, or to be erected on the North Side of the said River Ouze, shall be separate and distinct Gates and Turnpikes; and the several Tolls granted and made payable by the said former Act, shall be paid at such Gates or Turnpikes as are now erected or shall be erected on the said North Side of the said River Ouze.

And be it further enacted by the Authority aforesaid, That the Turnpike and Toll-house now erected at or near the Place called the Fryary, or Fryars, and also the Turnpikes at or near the Hassets and Saint Peter's in the Town of Bedford aforesaid, shall within One Month after the first Meeting of the Trustees, to be held after the passing of this Act, be pulled down, and taken away; and that no Turnpike or Toll-house shall afterwards,

during

during the Continuance of the said former and this present Act, be erected or set up at any Place between the Town of Elstow and one Mile North of the said Town of Bedford: And it shall and may be lawful to and for the said Trustees, or any Five or more of them, within one Month after the first Meeting to be held after the passing of this Act, to erect or cause to be erected or set up the said Turnpikes and Toll-house now standing at or near the said Places called the Fryary, or Fryars, and the Hassets, and in Saint Peter's in the said Town of Bedford; or any new Turnpike or Toll-house in, cross, or on the Sides of the Road by the said former Act directed to be amended, at such Place and Places, betwixt one Mile North of the said Town of Bedford and Westwood-gate in the said County of Bedford, as the said Trustees, or the major Part of them, at their first publick Meeting to be held after the passing of this Act, shall order and direct; and that all Persons travelling through the said Turnpike, shall pay the several Tolls granted by the said former, and continued by this present Act, notwithstanding such Person or Persons shall have paid the Tolls at any other Gate or Turnpike erected or to be erected between Elvestow otherwise Elstow aforesaid, and the Town of Saint Alban aforesaid.

Provided always, That nothing in the said former or this present Act contained, shall extend, or be construed to extend, to charge the Owners or Drivers of any Waggons, Carts, or other Carriages, carrying Corn, or any Sort of Grain to Market, on Market Days, either to the Town of Bedford, or the Town of Saint Alban aforesaid, with any of the Tolls or Duties granted by the said former Act, and hereby continued, such Waggons, Carts, or Carriages returning the next Day empty, the Owners or Drivers thereof producing a Note or Ticket, signifying that such Toll or Duty was paid for such Waggon, Cart, or Carriage the Night before; but if such Waggons, Carts, or Carriages shall return back the next Day loaded, in Nature of Back-carriage, then the Tolls and Duties shall be paid by the Driver or Drivers of such Waggons, Carts, and Carriages so returning back loaded as aforesaid; any thing herein contained to the contrary notwithstanding.

Exemptions from Tolls.

Provided also, and it is hereby declared, That all Waggons, Carts, or Carriages, going empty to the Town of Bedford over Night for Coals, or any other Loading, shall pass the next Day loaded Toll-free, the Owner or Driver of such Waggon, Cart, or Carriage,

producing

producing a Note or Ticket, signifying that such Toll or Duty was paid for such Waggon, Cart, or Carriage, the Night before.

No Turnpike-gate to be removed, except by Order of Trustees.

Provided always, and it is hereby also declared, That no Turnpike-gate or Toll-house which shall be erected cross or on the Side of the said Roads, by the said former or this present Act directed to be repaired after the passing of this Act, shall be taken down or removed, except by an Order of the Trustees, or any Five or more of them, made at a General Meeting of them, whereof fourteen Days Notice shall be given in Writing by the Clerk, under his Hand; which Notice such Clerk shall, and is hereby directed to give, by fixing, or causing to be fixed, on all the Turnpike-gates then erected on the said Roads; any thing in the said former or this present Act contained to the contrary notwithstanding.

Further Exemptions from Toll.

Provided always, and it is hereby declared, That nothing in the said former or this present Act, shall extend, or be construed to extend, to charge any Person or Persons with any of the Tolls or Duties by the said former Act granted, and hereby continued, who shall, from and after the said Twenty fourth Day of June, One thousand seven hundred and forty three, pass through any of the Turnpikes erected, or to be erected by virtue of the said former or this present Act, between Saint Alban's and Elstow aforesaid, with any Coach, Berlin, Landau, Chariot, Calash, Chaise, Chair, Waggon, Horse, Mare, Gelding, Mule, or Ass, Oxen, Sheep, Lambs, Hogs, or other Cattle whatsoever, which shall stop or stay at any Place or Places in the said Roads between the Towns of Saint Alban and Elstow aforesaid all Night, such Coaches, Berlins, Landaus, Chariots, Calashes, Chaises, Chairs, Waggons, Wains, Carts, Carriages, Horses, Mares, Geldings, Mules, or Asses, Oxen, Sheep, Lambs, Hogs, or other Cattle, passing before Twelve of the Clock the next Day, and the Owners or Drivers thereof producing a Note or Ticket, signifying that the Tolls granted by the said former Act, and hereby continued, had been paid on the Day before for the same respectively; any thing in the said former or this present Act to the contrary notwithstanding.

Lands chargeable to the Highways to continue so.

Provided always, and it is hereby enacted and declared by the Authority aforesaid, That if it shall appear to the said Trustees, or any Five or more of them, that any Lands, Tenements, or Hereditaments, or any Rents or Profits issuing out of any Lands, Tenements, or Heredi-

Hereditaments, now are, or hereafter shall be liable and chargeable towards amending any Part of the Roads by this Act directed to be repaired; such Lands, Tenements, and Hereditaments, shall still remain liable and chargeable; and the Possessors and Occupiers of such Lands, Tenements, and Hereditaments, are hereby directed and required to pay such Rents and Profits to such Person and Persons as the said Trustees, or any Five or more of them, shall appoint to receive the Tolls and Duties granted by the former Act, and hereby continued; and upon Default of Payment thereof, it shall and may be lawful to and for the said Trustees, or any Five or more of them, by Warrant under their Hands and Seals, to levy the same by Distress and Sale of the Goods and Chattels of the Person or Persons so liable to pay such Rents or Profits, returning the Overplus, if any be, to the Owner or Owners upon Demand, after all Charges paid; and such Rents and Profits, when recovered and received, shall be applied, from time to time, for and towards amending the said Roads, and to no other Use or Purpose whatsoever.

Provided always, and be it further enacted by the Authority aforesaid, That from and after the passing of this Act, all and every Person and Persons, who by Law are chargeable towards the amending the said additional Roads or Highways hereby directed to be repaired, shall, during the Continuance of this present Act, do and perform Three Days of that Work commonly called The Statute-work, which is appointed by the Laws now in Being for the amending the Highways of this Kingdom, in the said Parishes and Places, in which the said additional Roads or Highways do lie, in such Manner, and by such Rules and Methods, and under such Penalties and Forfeitures as in and by the said former Act is directed and prescribed, in relation to the doing and performing the Statute-work by the Inhabitants of the several Parishes through which the Roads directed to be repaired by the said former Act do lead. *Persons chargeable to the Highways to continue so.*

Provided also, and be it further enacted by the Authority aforesaid, That it shall and may be lawful to and for the said Trustees, or any Five or more of them, from time to time, during the Continuance of the said former and this present Act, to compound and agree with any of the Parishes to which the said Roads belong, or with any of the Possessors or Occupiers of such Lands, Tenements, or Hereditaments, as are or shall *Trustees may compound for Statute-work.*

be

be liable or chargeable to the repairing of any Part of the said Roads, for a certain Sum of Money, or otherwise by the Year, as the said Trustees, or any Five or more of them shall think reasonable, in lieu of the Statute or other Work to be done by such Parish or Parishes, or by such Possessor or Possessors, Occupier or Occupiers of such Lands, Tenements, and Hereditaments, chargeable as aforesaid.

Surveyors of Highways to agree with Trustees for Statute-work.

And to the Intent that proper Persons may be impowered to compound and agree with the Trustees for repairing the said Roads, for a Sum of Money to be paid by the Inhabitants of any of the Parishes, Townships, or Places, through which the said Roads intended to be repaired do lead, in lieu of their Statute-work to be done on the said Roads; be it further enacted by the Authority aforesaid, That from and after the passing of this Act, it shall and may be lawful for the Surveyor or Surveyors of the Highways of any of the said Parishes, Townships, or Places, with the Consent of the Inhabitants of such Parishes, Townships, or Places, first had at any Vestry, or other publick Meeting of the Inhabitants thereof, to compound and agree by the Year or otherwise, with the Trustees appointed, or to be appointed for repairing the said Roads, or any Five or more of them, for such Sum or Sums of Money to be paid by the Inhabitants of the said Parishes, Townships, or Places, in which the said Roads do lie, in lieu of the said Statute-work to be done on the said Roads, as the said Trustees, or any Five or more of them shall think fit; and in case such Composition-money so agreed to be paid, shall not be paid to the said Trustees appointed or to be appointed for repairing the said Roads, or to any Three or more of them, or to such Person or Persons as they, or any Three or more of them shall appoint to receive the same, within Fourteen Days after the same shall be demanded, it shall and may be lawful to and for any One or more Justice or Justices of the Peace for the County wherein such Parish, Township, or Place doth lie, and he or they are hereby required (upon Oath or Affirmation made before him or them of such Default of Payment) to issue a Warrant under his Hand and Seal, or under their Hands and Seals, impowering such Person or Persons so by the said Trustees, or any Three or more of them, appointed to receive such Composition-money, to levy the same by Distress of the Goods and Chattels of such Person or Persons as hath or have been made, or shall make such Composition for any Parish, Township, or Place as aforesaid, or of

the

the Surveyor or Surveyors of the Highways for the time being; and such Goods and Chattels so distrained, after the Space of Four Days (such Composition-money, and the several Charges of distraining and keeping the same not being paid) to sell, returning the Overplus (if any be) to the Owner or Owners thereof, upon Demand, after the Composition-money, and the reasonable Charges of Distress and Sale shall be first deducted; which Money shall go and be applied for and towards repairing the said Roads, and to no other Use or Purpose whatsoever.

Provided always, and be it further enacted by the Authority aforesaid, That if any Surveyor or Surveyors of the Highways of any of the Parishes, Townships, or Places, shall pay such Composition-money so agreed to be paid, or if the same shall be levied on him or them as aforesaid; he or they so paying the same, or on whom such Composition-money shall be so levied, shall be reimbursed the Monies so by him or them paid, or which shall be levied on him or them, in such Manner as the Surveyors of the Highways for the time being, are, by the Laws now in Being, to be reimbursed the Monies by them laid out and expended in buying Materials for repairing of the Highways. *How Persons paying the Composition-money shall be reimbursed.*

And be it further enacted by the Authority aforesaid, That from and after the Twenty fourth Day of June, One thousand seven hundred and forty three, it shall and may be lawful to and for the Trustees appointed or to be appointed to put the said former and this present Act in Execution, or any Nine or more of them, from time to time, during the Term or Terms by the said former Act granted, and hereby continued, by any Writing or Instrument under their Hands, without any Stamp thereupon, to borrow or raise any Sum or Sums of Money, at lawful or less Interest, on the Credit of the Tolls by the said former and this present Act granted and continued, in such Manner, and by such Ways and Means, as shall appear to them the said Trustees, or any Nine or more of them, most proper and convenient for the paying off the Money already owing on the Credit of the said former Act, and assigning the present Securities for the same, or making such other Securities as they shall think proper, for the effectual carrying on the Repairs of the said Roads, and compleating the same; so that the Sum or Sums borrowed and owing at one time on the Credit of the said former and this present Act, do not together exceed in the whole the Sum of Three thousand Pounds; *Money may be borrowed on Credit of the Tolls.*

which

which said Sum and Sums of Money so to be borrowed, and all such Sum and Sums of Money raised and collected, or to be raised and collected in pursuance or by virtue of the said former or this present Act, shall (after the Charges and Expences of passing of this present Act) be applied and disposed of, either in discharging such Sum and Sums of Money as is, are, or shall be due and owing on the Credit of the said former or this present Act, together with the Interest due and to grow due for the same, or for or towards amending the said Roads directed to be repaired by the said former and this present Act, and to and for such other Purposes as are therein and herein mentioned and expressed.

Turnpikes vested in Trustees.

And be it further enacted by the Authority aforesaid, That from and after the first Meeting of the Trustees, the Right, Interest, and Property of all and every the Turnpikes and Toll-houses erected or to be erected by virtue of the said former and this present Act, shall be vested in the said Trustees thereby or hereby appointed or to be appointed to put the said Acts in Execution; and they, or any Five or more of them, at their publick Meeting assembled, are hereby authorized and impowered to dispose thereof as they shall think proper; and to bring Actions, and to prefer Bills of Indictments, against any Person or Persons who shall steal, take away, break down, or spoil the same.

Justices impowered to act such, although Trustees.

Provided always, and be it further enacted by the Authority aforesaid, That it shall and may be lawful to and for any or either of the said Trustee or Trustees, who is, are, or shall be in the Commission of the Peace for the Counties of Bedford and Hertford, and also of the Town of Bedford, and Liberty of Saint Albans, to act as a Justice or Justices of the Peace in all Cases, Matters, and Things, that may be necessary for the more speedy and effectual putting in Execution the several Authorities and Powers in the said former and this present Act mentioned and contained.

Charges of passing the Act, &c. to be and paid.

And be it further enacted by the Authority aforesaid, That all such Costs and Charges as have been laid out and expended in, about, or by reason of procuring and passing the said former Act, or have been, or shall be laid out and expended in passing this present Act of Parliament, shall, in the first Place, be paid and discharged out of the Money collected or borrowed, or to be collected or borrowed by virtue of, or on the Credit of the said former and this present Act.

And

Anno Regni decimo sexto Georgii II. Regis.

And whereas it may be of great Service to have the Roads or Highways leading from the Town of Saint Albans to Luton, and from thence to Westwood-gate aforesaid, measured and divided into equal Proportions, by Stones or Posts erected or set up in or near the said last mentioned Roads, at the Distance of each Mile, or other Distances; be it further enacted by the Authority aforesaid, That the said Trustees appointed or to be appointed to put the said former and this present Act in Execution, or any Five or more of them, at any publick Meeting to be had after the passing of this Act, shall and may order and direct the said last mentioned Roads to be exactly measured, and Stones or Posts to be erected and set up near the Side of the said Roads, and thereupon denote the Distance of each Mile, or such other Distances as they shall judge convenient. *Roads to be admeasured, and Milestones erected.*

And be it further enacted by the Authority aforesaid, That if any Action or Suit shall be commenced against any Person or Persons for any Thing done or to be done in pursuance of the said former or this present Act, or in relation to the Premisses; every such Action or Suit shall be commenced within Three Months next after the Fact committed, and not afterwards; and shall be laid and brought in the County or Place where the Cause of Action shall arise, and not elsewhere; and the Defendant or Defendants in such Action or Suit to be brought, shall and may plead the General Issue, and give the former and this present Act, and the Special Matter in Evidence, at any Trial to be had thereupon, and that the same was done in pursuance and by the Authority of the said former and this present Act; and if it shall appear to be done, or that such Action or Suit shall be brought after the Time limited for bringing the same, or shall be brought in any other County or Place, that then the Jury shall find for the Defendant or Defendants; and upon such Verdict, or if the Plaintiff or Plaintiffs shall become nonsuited, or discontinue his, her, or their Action or Suit, after the Defendant or Defendants shall have appeared, or if upon Demurrer, Judgement shall be given against the Plaintiff or Plaintiffs, the Defendant or Defendants shall and may recover treble Costs, and have such Remedy for the same, as any Defendant or Defendants hath or have for Costs of Suit in other Cases by Law. *Limitation of Actions. General Issue. Treble Costs.*

Anno Regni decimo sexto Georgii II. Regis.

And be it further enacted by the Authority aforesaid, That this present Act shall be deemed, adjudged, and taken to be a publick Act, and shall be judicially taken Notice of as such by all Judges, Justices, and other Persons whatsoever, without specially pleading the same.

FINIS.

blank

blank

blank

blank

www.ingramcontent.com/pod-product-compliance
Lightning Source LLC
Chambersburg PA
CBHW082225220526
45470CB00010B/3310

TOKYO
ANOTHER GLANCE

喫煙ルーム ご用意しています

全席禁煙です

SANRIO RAINBOW WORLD RESTAURANT

サンリオレインボーワールドレストラン

17 more rows

List of named passenger trains of Japan - ...
https://en.m.wikipedia.org › wiki › List_...

About this result   Feedback

PEOPLE ALSO ASK

What is the fastest Shinkansen in Japan? ▲

"Nozomi (のぞみ, "Wish") is the fastest train service running on the Tokaido/Sanyo Shinkansen lines in Japan. The service stops at only the largest stations, and along the stretch between Shin-Osaka and Hakata, Nozomi services using N700 series equipment reach speeds of **300 km/h** (**186 mph**)."

Nozomi (train) - Wikipedia
https://en.wikipedia.org › wiki › Nozomi...

MORE RESULTS

Where is the Shinkansen station in Tokyo? ▼

How much does it cost to take the bullet train from Tokyo to Kyoto? ▼

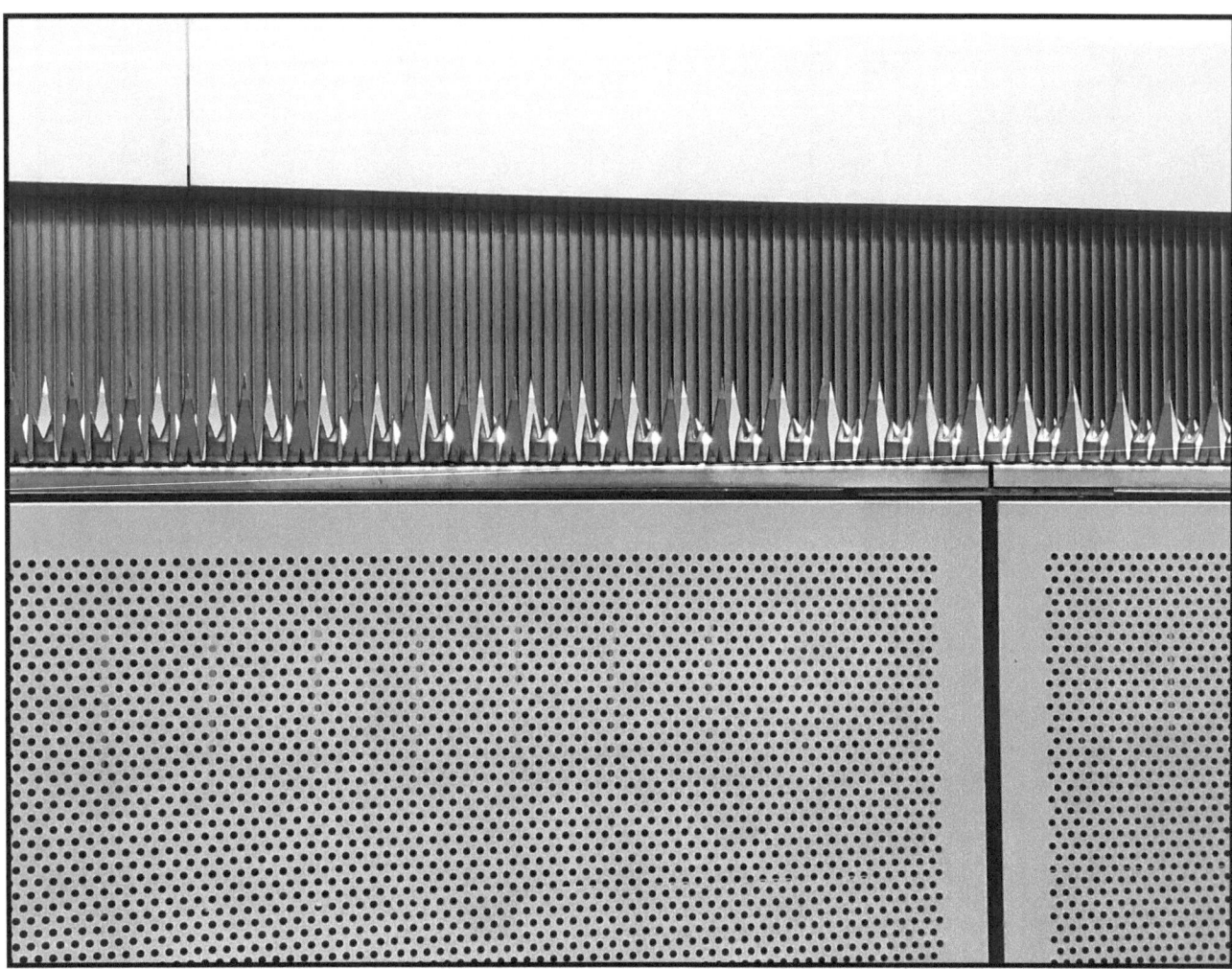

www.ingramcontent.com/pod-product-compliance
Lightning Source LLC
Chambersburg PA
CBHW051149220526
45473CB00003B/715